Affirmation Power
First Edition Affirmation Power copyright
March 1993
Author Michele Blood

Second Edition
The Magic Of Affirmation Power™
October 2019
Author Michele Blood

Published by MusiVation Int'l LLC
P O Box 12933
La Jolla California 92039
USA
All rights reserved.
Printed in the United States of America
ISBN: 978-1-890679-88-0

This book may not be copied, duplicated or used in any way without the written permission of the publishers.

For wholesale copies
of paperback and audio book versions
email team@TheMysticalExperience.com

Cover art by MusiVation™
Illustrations by Sanjay Adlink Malaysia

Dedicated to

*The Most Compassionate
Loving Enlightened Teacher*

Kundalini

TABLE OF CONTENTS

An Invitation 2

Introduction 3

My Life Changing Epiphany:
The Big Secret 5

What Is An Affirmation 10

What Do You Want? 14

Look At Your Thoughts 19

Money Is Energy 25

Visualization 28

The Power Of Meditation 36

Responsibility & The Solution 42

Fear and Love 45

Your Daily Action List 48

Gratitude & Appreciation 54

Competition 58

What is Consciousness 64

Affirmations 68

"Excellence is an art won by training and habitation. We are what we repeatedly do. Excellence then, is not an act but a habit."
- Aristotle

Shakespeare said, "All the world's a stage, and all the men and women merely players." Life is your own play. Today you can begin to choose happiness, success, perfect health, great relationships. All good can be yours. This is your life. Before you open the next page, make sure you have committed yourself to a better life by signing your acceptance to your New Life. Commit yourself to excellence. There is nothing stopping you. Fill yourself with joy, knowing that the next page you turn is your new beginning.

Turn to the next page of your new life.

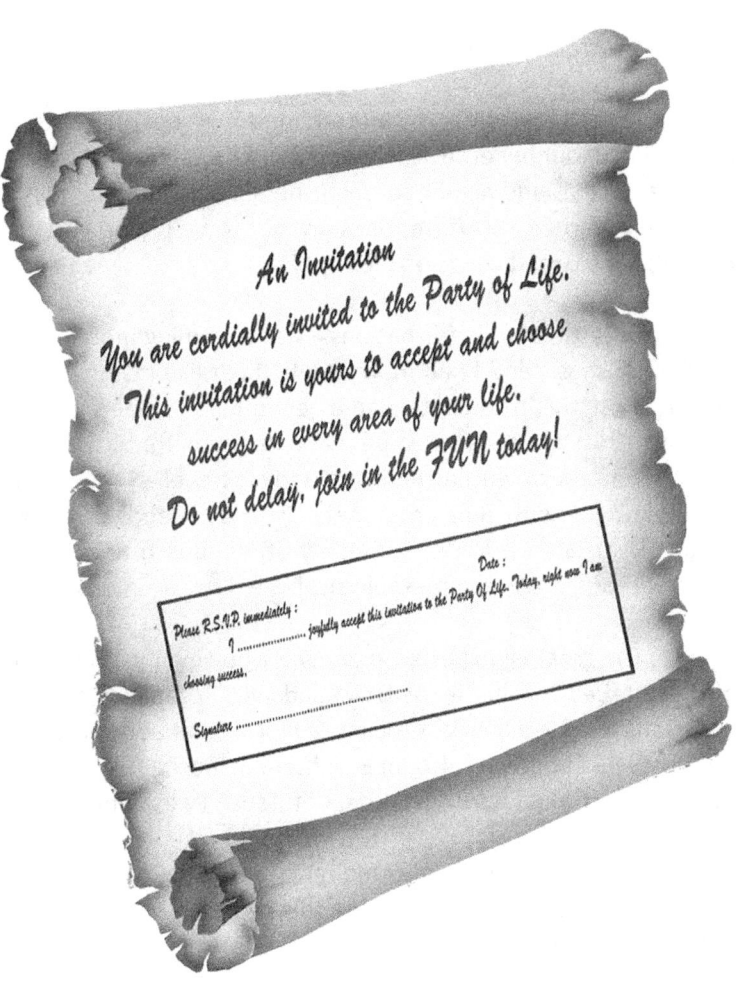

Introduction

I decided to update and re-release this book that I wrote back in 1993. I want people to understand the awesome power of affirmations, and that they can totally change one's life, especially when created through song.

When I first wrote my affirmation songs, not only was my body healed, but my entire life went into a new vibration of success, happiness, and higher consciousness. I began to have high, mystical experiences. Affirmations are not to be undervalued in their ability to uplift consciousness.

Because of the affirmations, I was becoming more aware in consciousness, and I had more clarity. I felt like my heart was glowing from the inside out. I had a newfound and deep love for the Divine. My life became so dear and beautiful that it was as if I had been reborn within the same body. I travelled the world, sharing stages with Bob Proctor, Louise Hay, Deepak Chopra, Wayne Dyer, Stuart Wilde, and many other superb teachers of positive thought and the metaphysical.

The greatest experience of my life however was meeting an Enlightened Teacher in the USA Kundalini. Because of my new consciousness I was, at last, being taught by someone who not only knew God but was also an Enlightened Teacher of such wit, humor, and compassion. A truly beautiful soul. I was home at last.

I began practicing my meditation more deeply than ever before, and it was possible because this beautiful Teacher transmitted Divine Light directly to her students. This high vibrating Holy Light, sometimes called Shakti, assists in awakening our own Kundalini. This transmission of Light makes one's spiritual journey oscillate at a much faster frequency than we could ever create on our own. It is a true gift from on High to meet an Enlightened Teacher who will agree to teach you and who speaks your language. Very rare.

I started after a few years studying with Kundalini to go through many beautiful Mystical Experiences, including what I call the Stargate Experience. I was pulled into this tunnel of Light and taken into different, higher dimensions. Eventually, my Kundalini awakened. It was not always easy, however the experience was worth everything to become free.

I now travel the world teaching and have beautiful people who are a part of what I now call The Mystical Experience # who are also uplifted and changed. Life becomes richer in all areas of one's life through raising consciousness. I know that none of this would have happened without first using the power of the affirmation music that I wrote to heal my body from a horrific car accident. May this book that is being re-released uplift your spirits and awaken you to new possibilities for your life's success, happiness and Enlightenment.

Always Remember: The Divine Presence IS with you.

www.TheMysticalExperience.com

Kundalini AKA Nicole Grace   www.LikeSwans.com

My Life Changing Epiphany: The Big Secret

"We are what we think. All that we are arises with our thoughts. With our thoughts, we make the world." The Buddha

The Buddha taught this over two and a half thousand years ago, so it's not such a big secret. With our thoughts, we create the world. You can use your thoughts through positive affirmations, visualization, meditation, and music. With the combination of all four methods, it only takes a few short months to turn your entire life to the positive.

I know you want a better, richer, and more successful life. I know this, for deep inside, we all do, and that is why I congratulate you. You are not one of the millions who sit at home night after night in front of the TV hoping and praying that one day, maybe if they win a lottery, if only this, if only that; everybody else is just lucky, they say. Do you know what luck stands for? Luck stands for learning and loving under correct knowledge. Statistics have proven that most people who win the lottery generally lose it quickly because they do not resonate with wealth in their consciousness, and so they were not prepared for such a large change in lifestyle.

When you are prepared in consciousness to accept prosperity and to be healed, then true positive change can be your experience. You are a magnet through your thoughts. Through changing your thinking, you can become as rich, healthy, and happy as you wish to be. You must decide you want a better life and then take the advice in this book. All it takes is you simply deciding. I know that nothing is impossible for you! I know this because I have experienced that nothing is impossible for myself. Allow me to now share with you how this all started.

I was a pop singer and songwriter in my native Australia and had a certain amount of success working six nights a week touring all over the country. I was persistent, and my bands were excellent. We worked hard. I co-wrote and recorded many, many songs; however, the big so-called lucky break seemed to elude me. I was persistent. I knew we were good. Our audiences loved us. We loved them. Why? Why wasn't the huge success I'd always dreamt of happening? What was the secret to success?

Then Bang! One night, on my way home from a gig, I was in a horrific car accident! My friend had fallen asleep at the wheel, and I, as the passenger, was crushed as the car hit a telephone pole. I had many injuries and broken bones, and I was told I would probably have numerous physical limitations. Many months passed in the hospital bed, and I underwent two very long major operations. I was very depressed, and I was in terrible physical pain.

A friend attempting to cheer me up gave me some motivational tapes to listen to, and as I was willing to try anything, I agreed to hear what they had to say. The first tape I listened to was Napoleon Hill's book "Think and Grow Rich". Hill said that he had healed his newborn sons hearing through autosuggestion. He spoke affirmations into his deaf son's ears every night for years. I thought if Mr. Hill healed his son, then I could also be healed.

I began speaking my affirmations out loud, however, it didn't seem to be working. Some teachers of New Thought have said that affirmations only work if you truly emotionalize the affirmations. I agreed at that time because I did not believe I would be completely healed. The doctors sure didn't say much. So, how were these affirmations ever going to work if I kept consciously rejecting them? I could not emotionalize that which wasn't true.

I would get disheartened and give up because of the physical pain I was experiencing from my many injuries.

I had a great thought one day that it would be easier to file the affirmations into my subconscious mind if I listened to them in song form. I asked my brother and some friends to please go and purchase some affirmation music. They looked everywhere, and there was no such thing as positive affirmations set to music. That is when my big epiphany hit me! I must write my own affirmation music. I then wrote my first affirmation song and recorded it on a little tape recorder right there in the hospital bed. *I Am Healed I Know I Am, I Love Myself I Am My Friend, As The Healing Light Of The Universe Surrounds and Goes Through Me, I Know That I Am Healed.*

Well, it worked. What the doctors thought was impossible became possible. My body was completely healed. It felt like a wonderful, magical, life changing, amazing, beautiful miracle.

As a singer and songwriter, I knew that once you have a jingle or pop song in your mind, it is there forever. The lyrics activate the logical left side of the brain, and the melody activates the right hemisphere of the brain, so you have a whole-brain experience. This way the conscious mind does not have an opportunity to reject the new thought. The affirmation plants itself as a positive seed into the subconscious mind. Then, the magic happens, and new trees of positivity begin to grow and fill our vibration with ideas of success, which then attracts to us, just like a magnet, wonderful experiences and healing.

I then realized what a HUGE EPIPHANY it was to put these affirmation songs to music. (Now called MusiVation™) What a moment of Satori. No one had done this before. It was a Divine Gift. I could see the reason that I was a singer and songwriter, and how my entire life had all lead to this moment. My purpose was now clear: to spread this music to the world, to release suffering, and release poverty consciousness. I was healed, and I was experiencing such joy and newfound success. To me, it was a miracle.

I am going to show you how, in very simple steps, to uplift your life experience. We are going to keep it simple and spiritual. As I always say, K.I.S.S., or "keep it simple and spiritual." In this book you will learn about the magic and power of affirmations combined with music which is the fastest way to begin to change your thinking to the positive.

I absolutely love my life now! All my dreams are continuously coming true. I have since created for myself a wonderful life, travelling around the world and experiencing a deep and meaningful life. God is truly good. I am becoming more awake and aware of this gift called life. It all started with a song that changed my life forever. Nothing is impossible. I am now walking perfectly and singing and teaching all over this beautiful world. I am a healthy, happy, and a very grateful soul.

I am going to gift you, for free, THREE of my favorite affirmation songs. I Am Healed, I Am A Magnet to Money and Step By Step I Will Persist Until I Succeed.
www.AffirmationPowerSongs.com

WHAT IS AN AFFIRMATION?

An affirmation is, an affirmation is, yes; it is something you say repeatedly. It is a statement of word, thought, feeling, or action which confirms a belief system or patterning that we hold in our subconscious mind. Now, these can be negative or positive. It's up to you to decide to choose negative or positive thoughts. For example, "I am miserable because my hair is falling out." Or, "I am now so happy because I no longer need my haircut." You see, it's all perspective. Your subconscious mind believes everything you tell it. The subconscious mind is subjective. If you tell it enough, it believes and manifests that thought and positive state of mind into your reality.

From now on, choose only positive statements. Repeat them over and over again. Your affirmations must always be stated in the now. Remember, the subconscious only knows now. If you say, "I wish to be rich and healthy," your subconscious will never know when you want it as you are only wishing. Instead say, *I am now! abundantly rich and healthy because I am earning more money every day and my income always exceeds my needs. Extra money comes to me every week through Divine Magical Happy Ways.*

You see, as far as your subconscious is concerned, everything is now. So, saying you want to be or you're going to be, or you wish to be, isn't now. You must always state it in the now, then set your goal and be specific.

Say right NOW:
*I am strong I am beautiful I only attract good in my life
I Am A Magnet to Money*

You become a magnet to what you are affirming. You are what you think about because thoughts become things. As you are reading this, if anything stands out, underline it. The more you understand, the more magnetic you become as your vibration quickens. When you use positive affirmations, you are feeding your subconscious with positive programming or conditioning. The process is simply planting good seeds of thought instead of bad. If you plant a strawberry seed, strawberries will grow. If you plant negative thoughts, only negative conditions will manifest.

Affirmations, as well as your goals, must be felt and believed. If they can't be felt and believed, use my affirmation songs or make up your own songs. It might sound repetitive, but I truly want you to get it, whatever your "it" is. Become magnetic with positive thoughts. Manifest your good now.

Singing along to musical affirmations is very powerful and so fast as every word plants itself straight into your subconscious mind. Even if you are simply listening to the music, allow it to go around and around in your mind. It is like, for example, a cat food jingle. Instead of hearing, "I love my kitty food," when you may not even own a cat, start singing to yourself the affirmation song I gifted to you earlier.

I AM A MAGNET TO MONEY
I NOW HAVE MORE THAN I NEED
I AM A MAGNET TO MONEY
Money Money Loves Me

I know what I prefer to be planting in my mind. Writing down your affirmations is also very powerful, as you are using most of your senses. Write these down a minimum of fifteen times every day, so that they will grow into a beautiful tree of prosperous thoughts. Write them in this book and whenever you need a lift, open and read. I have left some pages at the end of the book for your notes.

WHAT DO YOU WANT?

When you begin to write, listen, and sing your affirmations, make sure you are affirming what you want and not what you don't want. Here is an example, instead of saying, "I don't want to be fat anymore," say instead, *I am now at my perfect weight, looking good and feeling great!*

Create more joy and fun in your life. Life wasn't meant to be serious, and making money wasn't meant to be serious. Life is happening now, and you are here to enjoy every single moment. Your subconscious mind is a very obedient servant. Be clear that what you ask for is what you truly want to manifest. Otherwise, edit it from your mind. My good friend Bob Proctor has taught me a very quick and easy way to get a negative thought from the mind. Simply say, "Next!"

Next, affirmations are the foundation of your building. Think of it that way. The building is your goal, and your intention is to create. The affirmations support the building so that you can and will achieve all of your most loved goals. Continually feed yourself good thoughts, build up that foundation. You deserve the best! Say right now, *I am the best!*

"I _____ *am the best.*" Add your name.

Be careful of what you read. Don't allow other people to think for you. What you generally read about and hear in the news is unhealthy consumption. The truth is, there is far more good in this world than bad. If you were to interview people in the roughest and poorest neighborhood this very day, you would probably find they had a safe and relatively trouble-free day.

Most of what you read and hear in the news is magnified to sell. What do they say? Bad news sells. I'm telling you now that good news sells and will sell you on having a wonderful and exciting lifestyle. Only allow yourself to hear good news; be grateful, read positive books, listen to positive people, and positive music. Very soon, you will find you are attracting, just like a magnet, other positive people and positive opportunities. Actually, negative people may feel uncomfortable around you. Please never be concerned about what people think of you. Most people are only thinking about their own life, and not yours. As Terry Cole Whittaker says, "What other people think of me is none of my business."

You are a part of a universe that is abundantly unlimited. Therefore, being part of this universe, you are abundantly unlimited. Take a look at all the stars in the sky, the leaves on the trees, the grains of sand on the beach, as well as plants and animal life. We are living in absolute abundance. It is almost as if it were over-abundant. There is waste everywhere, and whoever told you that money doesn't grow on trees? Rubbish! Money does grow on trees. One form of money is what? That's right. Paper. What is paper made from? Yes, trees. Now other forms of money are gold, silver, copper, nickel, diamonds, opals, emeralds, and many more riches from our abundant Mother Earth. It is a recycling of nature into new energy forms and exchange.

Look at all that nature has to offer; The Divine does not skimp! We are all surrounded with abundance.

Feel grateful to The Divine and Focus on abundance. Write a gratitude list every night before going to sleep. The more you are grateful, the more you will attract what there is to be grateful for. It is a beautiful cycle of increase and joy.

When you start feeding your mind positive thoughts, you will attract creative ideas, perfect opportunities, and absolutely wonderful people. Yes, you become a magnet to all good experiences, including money. Then, the secret is to take action. When opportunities arrive, get up and take action. Then, and only then can you be a catalyst to show others how to experience the same. Be the example. Think about what you say. Know that you are creating your tomorrows with your thoughts today. Yes, I am repeating myself again for this is the so-called big secret. I love you, and I know you can do it. We are all from one mind. Feel the love I have for you and the love you have for yourself. We are from the same universe, and the same God of Love.

I also recommend you work out regularly as this will also raise your vibration and exercise makes one feel more positive.

Again, I am going to repeat myself. Only be with like-minded, happy, positive people. Go to seminars and workshops, and surround yourself in success. Surround yourself in abundance. If you must be with people whose energy is low or negative to you, change your thoughts about them. Everyone feels down sometimes, so have some compassion because the reason people get down is because they are in fear. You don't have to hang out with them, however, don't be so judgmental. We are all part of the omnipresent Divine. You will probably find as you change your thoughts about people, you will think they have changed. In reality, it is YOU who changes. Find something sincere to say to everyone, even if it is something as simple as, "How are the children?" or, "You're wearing a nice tie today." Everybody wants and needs to be acknowledged. So, begin today by acknowledging yourself. Say right now, "I acknowledge myself and know my thoughts are powerful." Write in your name:

I, _____acknowledge myself and I know my thoughts are powerful.

LOOK AT YOUR THOUGHTS

Please NEVER underestimate the power of the spoken word.

This may sound familiar. "In the beginning was the WORD and the WORD was with God. The WORD was God. And all things were made by the WORD. Without the WORD was not anything made that was made."

Here, the good book clearly teaches us that the physical universe is simply WORD in form. Jesus, Muhammad, Buddha, Vishnu, and many other great prophets said the same thing, just in different ways. "Do not judge, lest you be judged." "Love your neighbor as yourself."

The Divine Presence is so generous, giving, and loving, and lives within you. You are part of the loving Divine. The Divine in you is the same Divine in your neighbor. Before you can change the world, you have to change yourself. Change your thinking. We are what we think. It is our faith that heals us. It is what we believe. "What the mind of man can conceive and believe, he will achieve." Napoleon Hill stated that quite clearly.

What have you been creating in your life, with your spoken word? You are the co-creator of all. This news is happy. I want you to be happy with this news. You can now create all good into your life. Forget about luck. You create your own so-called luck. Don't look at any person, place, or thing as your supply. Trust and know that the Divine Eternal Mind, or whatever you choose to call your higher power, is the source of all your supply. So please, let go and let God. And remember, don't take life so seriously. SMILE!

As you sing, speak, and write your affirmations, always remember to smile. Show your teeth, gums, and all. Make your dentist proud. No matter how you are feeling, always remember to smile. It takes half as many muscles to smile as it does to frown. Look at yourself in the mirror. Make a funny face. SMILE! So, as you are singing and speaking your affirmations, stand in front of the mirror, dance around, and really let go. Dress up if you like. Shout it out. This is fun and extremely magnetic. Be fearless. Have fun on your way to riches. You are the creator of all your emotions. It all starts with a thought. It is changing your state of mind. Decide now to have happy emotions, and happy thoughts.

You must know at once and without any doubt that you are the one who is choosing fear, phobia, superstition, or sadness. Everything you created is through your previous thinking. If you want to know what thoughts you had yesterday, look at your life today, your body shape, your relationships, and your financial situation. How will your tomorrows look? Your body? Your relationships? Your finances? It's quite simple. You know the secret now! LOOK AT YOUR THOUGHTS TODAY. Emotions show up in the body as physical manifestations of your thoughts.

YOU MUST CHANGE YOUR THOUGHTS

YOU MUST BEGIN IMMEDIATELY, RIGHT NOW

Start singing a happy tune. Remember you and you alone must continually feed yourself positive thoughts. Condition yourself to exist at a higher level of excellence today than yesterday. Get your positive momentum going. It is like your body. You can't go to an exercise class just one day and expect to have a toned body. You have to be consistent. Society may predict, but only you can determine your destiny. Make your own conscious decisions. As Ernest Holmes said,

CHANGE YOUR THINKING

CHANGE YOUR LIFE

Positive changes can be created in moments. The level and emotions you feel can speed up your changes. That's why affirmations to music are so powerful. It helps to speed up the level of vibration. Willpower by itself is not enough; not if you want to achieve lasting changes. The affirmations in this book and on my albums are not only for yourself. Give them to your whole family, and even to your friends. We even have a special album of affirmation songs for young children. (I Can Do It. Positive Self Esteem Songs For KIDZ.) **Let your children sing along.** These young minds will be overflowing with good thoughts, and then they will create wonderful tomorrows. Be the role model, and everyone will want to learn your secret. You can tell them – it all started with a thought and a happy song.

Every morning as soon as you wake up, jump out of bed, stretch your body, and take twenty nice deep breaths in through your nose and out through your mouth. Be sure to exercise and meditate. Just get up one hour earlier. You will have more energy with less sleep. This will help you clear your mind to be ready for a bright new day. Feel the Divine life force flowing through you. Make a commitment to constantly improve yourself.

• SPEAK and SING your affirmations over and over.

• LISTEN to my singing affirmation MusiVation™ music.

• RECORD your own voice repeating your own personalized affirmations. This is POWERFUL.

• WRITE in this book your affirmations and goals. Be consistent. Be persistent, and you will succeed.

You are first class, and five star. It is your Divine heritage to have lots of money, and to have everything good in your life. Don't scare money away by saying that there isn't enough money. Treat your money well. Treat it well, and it will always come back multiplied. Get rid of the fear and guilt that money is evil. I believe that not having enough money for your family in order to provide food and shelter is far more evil than anything else. And to me, evil is just negative thinking, which exists by creating fear and negative situations.

I WILL PERSIST UNTIL I SUCCEED. I AM NOW BREAKING DOWN ALL BARRIERS IN MY WAY.

Money Is Energy

Money is simply energy. It is a force, and a power that is part of life, including the seen and the unseen, which is constantly moving and growing. Money in and of itself is not bad or good; it just allows us more FREEDOM.

So why do we get so crazy over this thing called money? Think of the ways we get consumed by money - we worry about having it, not having it, hoarding it, hiding it, and handing it to others. We lose our sleep, teeth, hair, friends, and sanity. We suffer from chronic seriousness over money. People who think about money the most are usually the ones who don't have much money. The most successful happy, wealthy people I know are continuously thinking of new and creative ideas and ways to uplift other people. Because of this, they're always attracting more money. They are people of action.

Even some people who have a lot of money become overly obsessed, and the result leads to unhappiness. I know you want balance in your life, and to be healthy, wealthy, and happy. Please do not listen to other peoples' opinions, especially from those who say that money is evil. That is not true. As I mentioned, money is simply energy. Don't infringe upon others by giving them your opinions. Honor others by keeping your mouth shut. Everyone is on their individual spiritual journey.

Be persistent! I know the magnificent spirit that you are. We all are from one mind; individualized creations of the Eternal Holy Light. Nothing is impossible with God. And as the beautiful Enlightened Mother Meera says so perfectly, "God wants you to have everything that will bring you happiness."

If one person can do it, then so can you. Remember to speak your affirmations onto your own special recording to add some personalization.

Say right now with feeling:

I AM BEAUTIFUL, I AM FEELING GREAT

I AM A MAGNET TO MONEY, I AM HEALED

You've got a lot of new programming to feed your mind. Know that from today onwards; your life is going to improve in every area. Life is a gift. Life is magical. You are magical. When you speak your affirmations onto your recording, please do your best to feel in a high vibration. Perhaps dance or exercise before you begin to record. Feel it. Tap your heart as you are saying your affirmations. Be consistent, write down your affirmations and goals. You are a magnet to good in all forms. Never give up, take action, GO FOR IT!

I AM A MAGNET TO MONEY.
I NOW HAVE MORE THAN I NEED.
I AM A MAGNET TO MONEY.
MONEY MONEY LOVES ME.

VISUALIZATION

Visualizing is fun because we allow our imagination to soar. The magnetic power connected to our imagination is powerful. Have fun with your visualization. Don't take yourself so seriously. This is your life and your dream. Be unlimited in your visualizing. Expand your imagination. You can be anything and everything you wish to be. Go for it. Most great athletes attribute their success to visualizing their way to success and swimming that final lap, being a winner. Which simply means always doing better.

Lee Evans, the four-time gold medalist in 1968, said, "I visualized every step of the four-hundred-meter race until I saw every step I would take." Another person who was a perfect example of visualizing was Walt Disney. He used all his imagination, seeing things even before they were built. Walt encouraged and supported all those who worked for him to start the day by affirming that they were using their creative imagination to achieve the best cartoons, then affirming, visualizing, and goal setting. When we use all three, lookout world, here we come.

Visualization is another powerful tool that utilizes the power of your mind to manifest into your experience resulting in a beautiful life. We can do this for other people as well. See your loved ones, happy and healthy and laughing. This is a very beautiful prayer. Please always remember to thank The Divine for going before you and going before your loved ones and preparing the way.

Let's share with you a real example from Bob Proctor and my own experience here in Malaysia. Bob and I have had many extraordinary things happen when we've used visualization. It's magical and fascinating. Our subconscious mind thinks in pictures and patterns. When we visualize, our subconscious mind doesn't know if it's real or not. Neuroscientists have proven this in recent years. If we see a photograph of a car, our mind thinks the car is an actual *real* three-dimensional object. The subconscious mind cannot differentiate between a real car and a picture of a car.

Here is our example. Bob and I were in Kuala Lumpur doing seminars and writing songs. We went to the middle of the city where they have a huge outdoor stage, and we were writing a song together called, *"Motivation for the Nation,"* which in Bahasa Malaysia is, *"Motivasi Untuk Bangsa."* We visualized we would have our song performed to an audience of *over* fifteen thousand and that this audience would also be singing along. We knew to add *over* because then we were not limiting the Unlimited Power. The thought of the Light and Power behind that many people singing together was *awesome.* It would be such a positive experience for all who were there. Now, remember, we hadn't even finished writing the song, let alone recording it. We were on the stage visualizing fifteen thousand people, and Bob always says that whatever you originally come up with, whether it's money or whatever, double it. So, we doubled it and said it was to an audience of *over thirty thousand*.

Move forward in time to New Year's Eve ten months later. There were three hundred musicians and dancers performing our song on that same stage to an audience of over fifty thousand people who were all singing along. Our song has been played on national radio, and the music video we created was on TV every day. The Prime Minister of Malaysia had chosen our song, by an Aussie and a Canadian, to help bring in the New Year for his country and yes, I repeat, there were over fifty thousand people bringing in the New Year singing our positive Light-filled song.

What I had done was to sing and record the song along with many of Malaysia's biggest singing pop stars, and it ended up being a very popular song. We sang it in the Malaysian language however I did also record it in English. It was sort of an anthem for Malaysia. That came about because of creative visualization. So, when you visualize, always see it happening now and do not ask how it will happen. Once you have decided on what you want and have visualized it, ideas and opportunities will arise. Then you take action on these ideas and opportunities.

Always ask for what you want or something even better, and always add, *I give thanks that this has happened in ways which were for my highest Divine good and the highest Divine good for everyone involved*, because the Infinite Intelligence knows what we want better than we know what we want and always knows the how to create anything and everything that will uplift our spirit.

We can become absolutely magnetic to such grace. We begin to oscillate at a very high frequency. The more we do this, then the more magnetic we become. Our goals literally cannot keep themselves away. Keeping it fun stops the sometimes-tedious nature of visualizing the same thing over and over. Expand your visualization. Add to it. Visualize happy experiences. Too many people get bored and give up. That is why it is important to encourage yourself to find joy and gratitude in all that you experience.

Decide to go for what you wish to achieve. No matter what your present circumstance is, your good can appear. At the right Divine place and the right Divine time, all will manifest.

At first, you may have some difficulty visualizing, and that's okay. A great tool that will help you is what I call Michele's Magnetic Future Self Board. Buy a large piece of cardboard or a poster board and draw a big magnet. In the magnet itself, write down your affirmations. Write on the top. I _____ (your name), give thanks to my Divine Higher Power, knowing that I am a magnet to all good. I see it. I feel it. It is now my experience.

Another gift for you is my audio program Michele's Magnetic Creative Visualization audio program AND the audio program by myself and Bob Proctor, Be Your Perfect Weight Looking Good and Feeling Great. Go to this link to receive your free gifts. www.AffirmationPowerGifts.com

Example of Michele's "Future Self Magnetic Board"
I_____give thanks to my higher power,
knowing that I Am A Magnet to all of this good

Inside the magnet, start pasting pictures of all the things you want to attract. Houses, cars, pictures of money, anything. In the middle paste a picture of yourself.

If it's weight you've been wanting to release don't say you want to lose weight, instead say, I am now at my perfect toned healthy weight. Cut out a picture of a body and paste your own face on it. This is very powerful. When I first got out of the hospital, I was painfully thin. I found a model in a magazine who appeared to be similar to my previous perfect weight. I pasted my own face on this model and looked at it every day, visualizing it was my new body.

After a while, I got the urge to exercise again. I started to gain weight and to eat the right kind of foods. Eventually, I got to where I am now which is my perfect weight. If it is weight that you wish to release again, I emphasize to never say you need to lose weight. You see, when the subconscious hears you say, "I am losing weight," then it goes into survival mode. The brain actually sends down endorphins to your body, so you actually get hungrier. The subconscious does not want you to lose anything from its precious body. So, I repeat, only say,

*I AM NOW AT MY PERFECT WEIGHT
LOOKING GOOD AND FEELING GREAT*

Before you know it, you'll get the urge to exercise. You'll soon be eating fruit instead of cake. The subconscious mind will make all of these attractive so that you will achieve your ideal weight. Your metabolism will begin to function to perfectly balance the food intake by slowing down or speeding up and all of this happens through your own mind.

Another example is a luxury car. Go down to the car dealers with your camera, dressed in your finest, and have your photograph taken sitting in the car of your dreams. Get a blank check. Write in your name and the amount of money that you wish to attract. Sign it, "The Universal Banker."

Continue to visualize yourself having the money, the houses, the holidays, and anything else your heart desires, knowing that you can achieve whatever you set your mind to achieve. Unique creative ideas will begin to flow and all that is required to support your vision will come to pass. We perform our own magic through our mind. Change your picture as your vision becomes bigger. Now move. Make it colorful and have lots of fun.

If you're unhappy with your career, your health could suffer, and it will be more challenging to achieve success. Even if you do achieve some success, you won't be happy. Life is here to enjoy, in every moment of every day. Sometimes we need discipline in our lives to achieve success, however, this is a good thing, for we use our will power. Discipline is not a dirty word. Visualize the outrageous. Be spontaneous. Don't just live a little; live a lot and go for it.

I am going to record this book, so a great idea could be to invest in yourself and purchase the audio version which will also have the affirmation songs and so much more. Then, you can listen to it repeatedly and plant new seeds that will keep you persisting until you succeed. www.MusiVation.com

I AM NOW AT MY PERFECT WEIGHT. LOOKING GOOD AND FEELING GREAT.

The Power of Meditation

Practicing Meditation forms the most important part of our work in becoming peaceful, happy, and connected to our Divine Presence.

I was on a beach in Sarawak East Malaysia recently, and as I sat down to meditate, I was gazing the waves, and I became one with the waves I was watching. I was the wave. Here I was in Malaysia, where I am now as I write this book, open and receptive to the Divine realizing the waves were me, and I was gone. The Eternal did indeed meditate me. Some people who are runners have had a similar experience. It is sublime and beautiful. Time stops.

The purpose of this book is to give you tools that will change your life by changing your thoughts. If that's true, then why speak about meditation which is meant to stop thoughts? Well, if we desire to move ahead and have success and good health flowing, we must continue to vibrate at faster and higher frequencies. The Divine Holy Light which is our Higher Self is the only true vibration. So of course, when we are going into the silence, we can connect with our true self and vibrate at higher frequencies. This is why I have what I call heart glow. Through meditating with focus on my heart chakra, the Divine within me has been activated. It is sublime. It is not always easy to begin to silence our mind, but it can be achieved. We have to practice tapping into that which sustains all of life.

The power of meditation is often overlooked. If you wish to truly connect with our Higher Self, then this chapter on meditation will assist you to look more deeply. This chapter will teach those who have never meditated before and will remind those who do practice meditation – its awesome power. When we practice meditation, we are consciously connecting, in the silence, to our Higher Power.

Although there are many ways taught to achieve silence through meditation practice, I will share with you some ideas that will meet your needs very nicely indeed.

I love to meditate in water, in nature, or on a beach; however, when we are meditating at home, I find it is best to create our own space where we will meditate. Clean this area well, as this will release old energies, because when we meditate it is best to have clean energy. Buy a brand-new mat on which to sit. Light a beautiful candle, as you can use the candle flame to focus your attention. A candle *does* bring good energy into your space as does traditional incense. A flower or a lush green plant is also good. If you do not live alone, ask your roommate or partner to please respect that this is your special place. Of course, to sit outdoors on the earth or on a beach is always energetically cleansing, but when at home, always designate a special place to meditate and meditate alone.

Meditation is not meant to make you sleepy; it is a focused practice. Visualization exercises are ok to do in bed as you can then flow into a positive sleep, filled with pictures that you can take into your dream time however meditation is not for relaxation, even though you will feel more harmonious. It is a very focused practice.

Once you have your meditation space prepared and cleaned, sit down on your mat, lotus style if you can, sit up straight, arms out to your sides and breathe in through your nose deeply, hold it and then exhale slowly through your mouth. Keep doing this until you feel peaceful. As you are now sitting peacefully, place your attention centered somewhere between the eyes and a little above. Next, take some word that is powerful to you, and you will know if it is powerful to you when you try some words out. LOVE, BLISS, GOD, SPIRIT, BEAUTY are good options. Ponder the word you choose. Some of my mantras are, *As a wave is one with the ocean I am One with God, As a ray of sun is one with the sun I am one with God, I Love God, or God's Grace is flowing through me, I am now a clear instrument for God's Grace, or AUM*. Use only one power word if that suits you better. You do not have to be religious to do this. Meditation is about focus and connection as a means to strengthen your mind. Replace the word God with Love if this feels more comfortable to you. I also love to listen to some Mozart because I find this keeps my mind still.

As you're sitting and focusing on your power word, Love, Heart, etc., your thoughts *will* wander off. When this happens gently refocus your mind back to the same mantra or word. Feel no impatience with yourself or frustration. No matter how many times your mind wanders, bring it back to that one word.

If you do this simple method, eventually, you will find that intruding thoughts will cease, and you will be able to sit quietly in a peaceful state. It may take days, or it may take months to acquire this steadiness of mind, but it will come if you have patience and are consistent.

At first, do not attempt to remain quiet for more than ten minutes or so unless you feel like it. After a couple of weeks, meditate for twenty minutes, and so on until you can sit comfortably for much longer periods. We are doing this to have a conscious realization of our unity with Spirit or to make contact with God. Keep it simple. KISS – "Keep It Simple and Spiritual," and remember to smile as we wish to bring a happy vibration to our meditation. I call smiling my *Happy Meditation*.

After ten to thirty minutes of meditation, and after you have achieved that feeling of peace, joy, and unity with the Universe, give thanks, get up, and go about your day. Please do this twice a day early am, and I love to also meditate at sunset and midnight when all is so quiet.

Even if you are agnostic, look at meditation as physicians do. It has been documented that people who meditate regularly have low blood pressure and generally are healthier, happier human beings. So, do it even if the word God is not your thing. Put a smile on your face as you sit down to meditate, as this does help your mind find peace. Do whatever you can to put yourself into a happy mindset before you sit down.

As mentioned, this chapter is a simple way of learning to practice meditation. Before we truly experience real silence, we are all only practicing meditation. But every time we do this, we do raise our consciousness, even if we do not realize it. In time, we will feel better and clearer, as well as less clogged or stressed. Please do not begin this practice with an overly serious tone. Focused? Yes, but not so serious. Oscar Wilde said, *"Life is too serious to be taken seriously,"* so lighten up! Focus your attention and feel happiness and gratitude. This way, it is a simple and easy way to begin to practice, but do not underestimate its power. If you do not at first feel any connection or peace of mind, that's fine. Just having the intention to consciously connect and feel the presence of God will eventually create peace, joy, harmony, and everything good will begin flowing your way.

WHY?

Because at least for a few minutes a day, you have chosen to get out of the way and let God in. As you delve into longer meditations and find a way that suits you best -and there are many different ways to learn meditation- your life and health will radically change for the better. Oh, yes, it will.

If you are having a hard time with your meditation practice, do not give up, and allow these loving and all-wise words by the great soul Paramahansa Yogananda to assist you: "*Your trouble with meditation is that you don't persevere long enough to get results. That is why you never know the power of a focused mind. If you let muddy water stand still for a long time, the mud will settle at the bottom, and the water will become clear. In meditation, when the mud of your restless thoughts begins to settle, the power of God begins to reflect in the clear waters of your consciousness. You will become a smile millionaire.*"

Yogananda's books were my first lessons in meditation. I highly recommend you read, "Autobiography of a Yogi." I must have read it twenty or more times. Yes, let us become Smile Millionaires! Always remember to smile sincerely and breathe. Life is magical, oh yes, it is! Say right now:

Life Is Magical, and I Am Magical

Here is another free gift.
The video
The Power of Meditation
www.AffirmationPowerGifts.com

RESPONSIBILITY AND THE SOLUTION

I have realized that the more my vibration rises, then the more responsibility I can accept. I am becoming stronger in spirit, and this will also happen for you. Fear is not as common now. We become brave, and even when we do feel fear, we take action and the fear disappears. Fear is a lie pretending to be the truth. The secret to becoming responsible is to always look for the solution to any challenge. The solution will always come. Just be still, breathe, and await the Omniscient Divine to guide you.

If we run away from any challenge, we have to repeat it. When we take immediate action with our responsibilities, we can ride the energy, and then it is much easier to complete tasks harmoniously. Do not wait until the last minute, as this creates stressful situations. We must face each challenge head-on and find the solution.

We must be brave, and this takes a lot of honesty. We have to take self-inventory and not judge anyone or anything for any challenge. Take responsibility and work through it, courageously.

Believe and trust in yourself. What matters is what you believe, what you think. Ask yourself honest questions. Empowering questions will manifest the answer, and the truth will be revealed.

At this point, the secret is to take action and look at the positive. Look at what you have learned. This way, you will grow in self-confidence and in every area of your life. You may find there are a lot of old records of negativity playing in your head. Taking action and being responsible will stop all that negative self-talk. Your Higher Self is always there for you, twenty-four seven. We are never alone. Know that every answer will open itself to you whenever you ask. Especially when we quit blaming other people and outer circumstances for our life. Affirm the real truth.

Affirm right now:

I AM A POWERFUL SPIRIT LIVING IN A PHYSICAL BODY
I NOW OPEN MYSELF TO THE SPIRIT WITHIN KNOWING THAT
THE ANSWER IS RIGHT WHERE I AM
I Am Open And Receptive to receive all solutions

Open your mind. Listen to your inner voice. It will always quietly guide you to your highest good. When everything appears to be going wrong, know that the solution is there and has always been there just waiting for you to ask the right question.

So, ask and say with full responsibility: *What can I learn by this experience? How can I improve? Why did this challenge appear?* I repeat, only ever look within, and then we can learn and grow.

Maybe the next book you open or the next person you meet will open your door of opportunity. The solution is right where you are. Do not run and hide. You can't hide for it hides within you waiting to manifest again.

I AM NOW DEVELOPING MY MIND WITH FURTHER EDUCATION.

FEAR AND LOVE

FEAR

Fear is the cause. The effects of fear can be:
Anger
Guilt
Loneliness
Blaming others
Jealousy
Resentment
Becoming Reactionary
Hate
Pride
Greed
Cruelty
Panic
Anxiety
Being Judgmental
Dishonesty
Self-justification
Depression
Envy
Theft-Coveting
Self-Pity
Murder
Demanding
Urgency

Ask yourself what the real cause of these effects/behaviors are. They are all the effect of the original cause, which is FEAR.

LOVE

If LOVE is the Cause, then the effects
of love which is the opposite to fear could be:

Peace
Self-acceptance
Feeling one with The Divine
Responsibility
Freedom for all life
Being Happy for another's good
Love
Humility
Kindness
Calm
Acceptance of others
Being Open and Honest
Trust
Generosity
Compassion
Joy and self-expression
Honoring others
Knowing the Universe is our Supply
Inner Strength
Loving all of Life
Giving
Tranquility
Self-Love
Affection
Respecting All People
Joy

I AM NEVER LONELY. FOR I AM MY BEST FRIEND

The Power Of A
DAILY ACTION LIST

It has been scientifically proven in research studies that people who write down their goals achieve them. When we also add the power of the mind through Affirmation Power, then a planned daily action list will make us unstoppable. It seems so simple; however, not many people will stick to a plan or even write down any goals. Create a BIG GOAL and every day you work, follow a positive action list. If you took action on even just one idea that you have received in this book, your income will increase, and your life will improve. So, imagine how much you can attract and create if you followed all of these ideas? WOW!

You will become Irresistible to
Money, Happiness, Health and Success

If you were told that if you make this daily action list every single day for the next thirty days, there would be a pot of gold waiting for you and your dreams would come to life, would you do it?

I am sure that you would. But many people say they will and then after a few days give up. Be one in the 3% group who NEVER GIVES UP.

When you first begin making a daily action list, you will find that projects in the past which once seemed impossible can now be completed and *ahead of time.* Your life will begin to have clarity and order, and your success will begin flowing. You will be able to accomplish more with less time. No more doing things just to be busy. Doing this list WILL help you in ways that will seem miraculous.

Instructions

Write down your daily action list at night. You will do your daily list every evening for thirty days. Why write your list in the evening? This is because as you are sleeping your subconscious mind will help you attract opportunities and creative ideas for those actions to come to fruition. It will help you be self-propelled to take positive, enthusiastic action the next day.

Highlight each action that is completed with a bright yellow highlighter after each task is completed. I recommend you write down the hardest action first. You will find that making that call you have been putting off early in the morning after you have meditated and completed your spiritual practices will no longer cause you anxiety. Calling anybody for any reason will now seem like fun. Doing the actions that you don't like or that intimidate you *first* will help you gain light, self-confidence, and power. *You know:* those things that you keep putting off.

Research has proven that doing this will accelerate your goals to fruition faster than you could ever realize. You will no longer be a procrastinator; you will be a doer, not a wishful thinker. A quickening of good will begin to appear in your life. If you have not completed the six items on your list by the end of the evening, add what was not completed to the next day's list. Do not beat yourself up, if you haven't done them all. Say to yourself,

This is so simple. It is worth it to me. I will have clarity. I will know what I've done. I will stay clear. I will be getting things done that are helping me achieve my dreams towards success. I am committed to taking these positive actions on my daily action list. I know that each detail is just as important as any other.

You know the saying: *God is in the details.* Do each action with total focus and impeccability. Taking each action with love, focus, and impeccability will also keep you mindful. If you find you are not doing all of the things on your DAILY LIST, perhaps you've put up one action step that is too complex to be one action. This is not goal setting; these are actions to help you complete your goals.

Here is an example of a goal as opposed to an action: *Today I will create a website and put a streamed video of me on my website for customers to get to know me and learn about our wonderful services.* This is a goal, and not an individual action. Instead, I recommend one action towards this website goal could be, *Buy domain name today* for the next day, *Find web designer,* for the following day, *Get a photograph of myself looking positive and happy for the homepage of my web*site, for the fourth day, *Hire a camera and video myself sharing who I am and how my service has so many benefits,* for the fifth day *Have a video compressed at local video editors to add video to my website,* and the sixth day *Write copy for the home page,* etc.

Are you beginning to understand how this works?

Now with this example, it could take a week to a month working on the preliminary action steps for completing your Website.

Can you see how working with a daily action list can help you achieve any project your mind can imagine? You don't list a project as one item on your DAILY LIST. Instead, break it down into action steps.

By breaking down your goals into manageable pieces, you will find that your six tasks will be very easy to do. Please don't overwhelm yourself by putting more than six items on your DAILY LIST. Just do one thing at a time.

The reason I have indicated a numbered day, thirty in total, for each DAILY LIST is because you will want to make sure that you make this list every single day for a full consecutive thirty days. That's right: seven days a week. This way, it will become an easy thing to do and will no longer feel like a discipline. It will be just as easy as brushing your teeth and showering. It will become a new, positive habit. After the initial thirty days, you can do perhaps just four or five days a week if that is what you choose to do. That being said, when making this list for the first time, it is recommended that you begin with a consecutive thirty days. Then, you will have created a new positive paradigm and increased your clarity and your results will be exponentially more successful. Plus, you will feel so confident and good about yourself.

If you do miss a day, start over from day one. Even if you are on day twenty-five and you miss one day, begin again at day one until your full thirty days has been completed. You may be up to day twenty-eight and miss it because of just feeling like you deserved a day off; however, that is simply an old paradigm sneaking back in. Forgive yourself and begin again at day one.

Soon this will become a new habit that you will find gives you deep satisfaction and inner fulfilment. Yes, you will see definite positive results. You will know that this initial thirty days was well worth it as you will be so ahead in the game of life that it will feel miraculous. You will have so much achieved. You can do this. Do it for you!

Please do not cheat by making any justifications as there is no point in cheating yourself. This is your life, don't waste it. You are the one who is responsible for making your life awesome.

You deserve this for you. Be enthusiastic and begin day one of your daily action list. I suggest you add one more thing to your list, *today I serve another*. You can serve another through a tithe, an act of kindness, a gift, a smile to a stranger etc.

*Go to this link to receive another gift of Michele's Turbo Charged Daily Action Planner **and Bob Proctors** audio program ACTION.*
www.AffirmationPowerGifts.com

Example of a DAILY LIST ~
for: _____
(date)

I am so enthusiastic and happy about becoming focused and doing my positive daily action list. I know that taking these actions is definitely helping me achieve my goals.

I LOVE doing these positive actions. It is easy for me to do my daily list one positive action at a time.

Positive Action #1

Positive Action #2

Positive Action #3

Positive Action #4

Positive Action #5

Positive Action #6

Gratitude & Appreciation

Gratitude is one of the most powerful forces in life because it is one of the many facets of love. When we understand this, we find that gratitude will play a far greater role in creating happiness and success than can ever be understood.

The mistake most of us make is that we are only grateful for the good that *comes to us* instead of having gratitude for the good *we have now* and for that which *we do want* before it appears. Let's find a deeper appreciation of all the so-called little things in life.

Take breathing, for example. Breathing is something we take for granted. Be grateful for the fact that we can breathe without having to think about it. Some are not so fortunate. You can also write out on sticky notes thank you God messages and put them all over your house hide them in books etc.

Let's do a simple exercise right now to get into a place of gratitude and appreciation. Make a list of things and people right now that you are grateful for and what you appreciate. The power behind being grateful and being appreciative is beyond our human comprehension. It creates miracles and enormous success. Wonderful opportunities will seem to fall out of the sky into your lap.

Remember, success without fulfilment is empty and meaningless; *with* fulfillment, success is pure bliss. So, remember to always be grateful and appreciate all that you receive and experience. I mean everything. Every night before you go to sleep write in a special exercise book or note pad at least six things or people you were grateful for that day. Anything from having a hot shower, to arriving safely at a destination, a smile some stranger gave you, or perhaps the name of a friend you appreciate who is in your life. Put a date on each page and at the end of the week read them all out loud. It is a very powerful exercise and will stop you from indulging in *pity parties.* PLUS you will attract even more things to be grateful about into your life.

I, _____, give thanks for all of this in my life and more. Thank you Divine for these and even greater experiences in my life. I know Divine that you have gone before me to prepare the way,

- _____

- _____

- _____

- _____

- _____

- _____

- _____

COMPETITION

Another topic I would like to share with you is competition. I am adding this topic because comparing one's self to others is very common and can be disheartening. Also, certain people feel they need to be on top of the opposition, other companies, and other people. You are your own individual unique wonderful manifestation of The Divine, so, please stop putting yourself into competitive states of mind. It is extremely disempowering. There is no need for it. All it does is to lead you down the not so merry path of comparison. You are unique. Just as two flowers may be different, each is equally as beautiful. Look at the rose, then at the orchid. Look at two puppy dogs; a poodle and a cocker spaniel. Both are cute dogs, yet they are very different. There is no competition, it is simply preference.

All that competition stuff just gets us into, "Whose daddy has got the best job," syndrome. Who cares? Get off it. Just be the best version that you can be of you. All you can do is better yourself. To really empower yourself, only be in competition with yourself. Better yourself every day. Say right now, *every day in every way I am getting better and better.* This is a powerful affirmation. Say it again, *every day in every way I am getting better and better.* The most successful athletes only ever compete with themselves. They set higher goals than the goals they achieved yesterday.

Be a winner in your own life. Winners better themselves. They visualize themselves always doing better. Business corporations that try to put other people out of business or treat everyone as competition are on the path of self destruction. They can never achieve peace of mind and true success that way. Businesses that sustain and maintain success achieve this by only being in competition with themselves. They love their customers and always look at what can be done to improve productivity, creative ideas and excellence. These businesses treat their employees with individual respect and love. Everyone's contribution is valid, and all are encouraged to be creative. These companies thrive in so called recessions. They are magnetic to success. True winners in their own game of life.

Here is an example of setting the goal and ignoring so called competition. In 1977, Jan Jacque, a rock and roll promoter, was driving through a snowstorm in New Jersey. Unable to go any further, he stopped at a banquet hall. There was a band on stage, and only three people in the audience. Jan sat next to Rocky the owner and told him if he had a place like this, it would be packed every night. Right there and then, Rocky made the decision that Jan could have the door cover if Jan paid the band. The name "Rocky" reminded Jan of a famous cartoon "Rocky and Bullwinkle". From that night, Jan decided to rename the banquet hall to the club title of "Bullwinkle's."

Jan did not look around or study other so-called competition on the club circuit. He simply visualized the club packed with people. The only means he had to publicize "Bullwinkle's" were flyers and action steps. Never for one moment taking his focus from his goal. He continually visualized the room packed with happy people. He revamped the interior with his original plan of expansion. The club went from a seven-hundred-person capacity to a one hundred and nine-acre area, full scale night club extravaganza with an opening night of over seven thousand people. Dozens of major night club owners frequented his phenomenal success. Some became so worried that they dissipated their energy through fear. In the eighties "Bullwinkle's" was still one of the largest nightclubs in the world. Jan Jacque did it without looking at any other competition, keeping his vision, knowing and having faith that it would be done, continually visualizing the room packed with people.

Study people's successes, and not their failures. Visualize yourself as a success. You could learn far more from people's successes than their failures. The old saying, learn from other people's mistakes, is rubbish. You can learn so much more by studying success. If you are to learn from your own mistakes, learn by not repeating them. Build up an even higher prosperity consciousness by only being with people who are successful and prosperous and who have success consciousness. It doesn't necessarily mean that your friends or your good self have the money right now. However, if you and your friends have the consciousness, believe me sooner or later, you will also have the money.

Even if you are down to your last dollar, invest it wisely. Go to the most expensive hotel in town. Sit in the hotel lobby. SEE and FEEL the prosperity and abundance all around you. Know that this is your Divine Heritage. Put on your best clothes, feel good, look good, visualize staying in this 5-star hotel.

You have far more opportunities meeting someone here who can support and strengthen your success than in a greasy spoon. Say now I am 5-star First Class. This is not about ego it is about raising your consciousness and living a purposeful fulfilling life. Come on visualize it, say it. Really mean it.

I AM A 5 STAR FIRST CLASS

Visualize yourself continuously being, having, and doing all you can to raise your consciousness. Expect the best and you will get the best. Imagination is a powerful tool, plus it is fun to use. See and feel yourself in prosperity. If your clothes are made of cheap materials, then imagine they are made of pure silk. If it is cheap shoes that you are wearing, imagine they are of the finest leather. Visualize it, imagine it.

Even people who go through times of not having money know that money is just around the corner if they have prosperity and success consciousness. You can't dress up a street person in great clothes and expect this person to attract money if they are still in poverty consciousness. The best way to succeed is for that person to start building prosperity consciousness and to have a major goal and intention to improve. They will have to feel it and see it in their mind's eye. It all starts with a thought. We think in pictures. That is why using our imagination is so powerful as we can update the image.

A good example of this is from a friend, Sloane Wooldridge, who is an actress in California. When auditioning for a part as a nun, Sloane does not need to dress in nun's clothing. She is already in the habit by believing and visualizing herself as a nun. She believes that she is a nun. In her mind's eye she already wears the HABIT. Sloane is the nun through the use of her imagination; the practice of acting and believing in herself.

Until you have built up your imaging skills, dressing up will really help your mind to believe that you have already achieved your goal. Always dress in your very best. People will suspiciously wonder what your secret is. You can tell them, "YOU GOT INTO THE HABIT."

Now, I would like you to take a few minutes to magnetize yourself to your true goals. Sit down somewhere quiet and close your eyes.

Take a nice deep breath through your nose and out through your mouth. Take another nice, deep breath. Now in your mind's eye, imagine that you have wings. Spread your wings and fly. Fly over mountains and streams, around high-rise buildings and big cities, and over the ocean. Look around and feel the freedom; breathe in the feeling now. Look down. What do you see? You see everything and anything that you wish to see. Visualize from the air your beautiful new home. Can you see it? Look at the beautiful land surrounding it. Isn't it gorgeous?! This is your new home. Look at it; look at the car parked in the driveway. What sort of car is it? This is your car. Fly around your home now. Take a good look. Take a moment to really see your beautiful home. Now come to a landing. Take another deep breath. Now let's have some fun. Right in front of you is a great big pile of money. I want you to take off at a fast run and nosedive into your money. Have a moment to play around, just like a child would. Now, visualize yourself with this money. See yourself taking it to a car dealer and buying your car and affirming that you own everything and that you are debt-free. Do this often.

Now congratulate yourself as you have begun the process of drawing to yourself all that is good. See yourself as the healthy person that you would love to be. Picture yourself loving your customers. Visualize things before you do them. Before you go to the banker, see it in your mind's eye, a perfect and fruitful meeting. Envision yourself making that sale. Have a wonderful time, knowing that you are creating fabulous tomorrows. Affirm now:

I Am Grateful For The Divine Presence Has Gone Before Me To Prepare The Way

What is Consciousness?

We have been talking a lot about prosperity consciousness, but what *is* consciousness?

Soul or Consciousness is our Higher Self. Joel S. Goldsmith said it perfectly, *"The day will come when, if you know enough about Consciousness you can leave everything else alone, for in the word, 'Consciousness,' and the spiritual understanding of it, is contained all the knowledge that is to be known about God, man, and the universe."*

We who are on the spiritual path, or seekers, are always doing all we can to raise our *consciousness.* Again, that word? When we speak of raising our awareness or raising our consciousness, we are doing our best to consciously connect with God so that we will eventually become awakened and free. No more duality. We may know it intellectually, but we don't know *it* unless we can *feel it* within. We are always striving to have more and more moments of pure bliss and knowingness. Transmissions do go on, and as we raise our awareness, we slowly begin to melt away the ice and begin to feel our connection with Spirit. Oh, our beautiful soul, what tales it shares when we are ready to listen.

That is when we truly begin to understand *that God is closer to me than breathing, closer than hands and feet. The Divine Eternal is inseparable and indivisible because we are one.*

Whether we believe this or not, that does not stop it from being true. Those who live in this realization *consciously* find that when any form of lack or so-called opposition comes into their experience, no fear enters and there is always a solution. This is Divine Truth, and the secret of the spiritual life. I am not speaking of religion, even though all religions do agree on this one point that *wherever we are, God is present.* When we meditate, we are doing this to connect with our higher consciousness or soul. In the silence, this is where true consciousness is experienced. This is where we are alive in Spirit. Our inner vision begins to open, and we hear, or feel, *the still, small voice* of our soul. These are the true eyes that see. Some have been able to see with their eyes closed when in a meditative state.

This *still, small voice* is our spiritual guide, and it goes beyond what we *think* intuition is. True consciousness has no thought. It is pure knowingness. If we wish to begin to gain a more conscious connection with our Divine Presence, we must meditate, which is why I added the chapter on basic meditation. Until we are in the silence, we are only practicing meditation. In today's world, there are over seven billion minds thinking, and we are taking on *their* thoughts. Without going into the silence, we can find it very hard to focus our mind, and this is one of the main reasons we get so stressed out and do our best to slip into something more comfortable like a collective coma by distracting our minds with hours upon hours of mesmerizing TV.

Most of the world is in a collective coma, which is also sometimes called the maya, and most people don't even know. They think they are awake. Fear and lack do not live in pure consciousness it only lives in duality.

One simple way to see whether we are rising in consciousness is to notice if we are becoming less reactionary. When we react, our ego still has dominion over our lives. When we notice that we are now witnessing life rather than reacting, we are gaining awareness. Respond, be in the moment before we react, and then our actions that follow will be right actions.

Another quote from Joel S, Goldsmith," *If, on entering a new year, our consciousness is the same consciousness with which we came into the previous year, we can be sure of duplicating the previous years' experience. But if our consciousness has deepened our New Year will be enriched."*

That says it all. Perhaps if Joel had been here at this time on the planet, he would have also mentioned the film "Groundhog Day," for without more awareness or higher consciousness we DO live our life and each year the same way over and over again. The names change, but the experiences remain the same. We, however, do not have to wait until a New Year rolls around to begin. We can begin right here and right now. Begin to meditate, do your affirmations, stop watching so much TV and focus on Light and on conscious union with God. Indeed, it is ALL about consciousness, and I will say it again... Remember to smile and always to be grateful.

Thank you for reading.

You are loved.

The Divine Presence is with you.

THE FOLLOWING PAGES ARE SOME POWERFUL AFFIRMATIONS

PLEASE REMEMBER TO ENJOY THE EXTRA FREE GIFTS AT

WWW.AFFIRMATIONPOWERGIFTS.COM

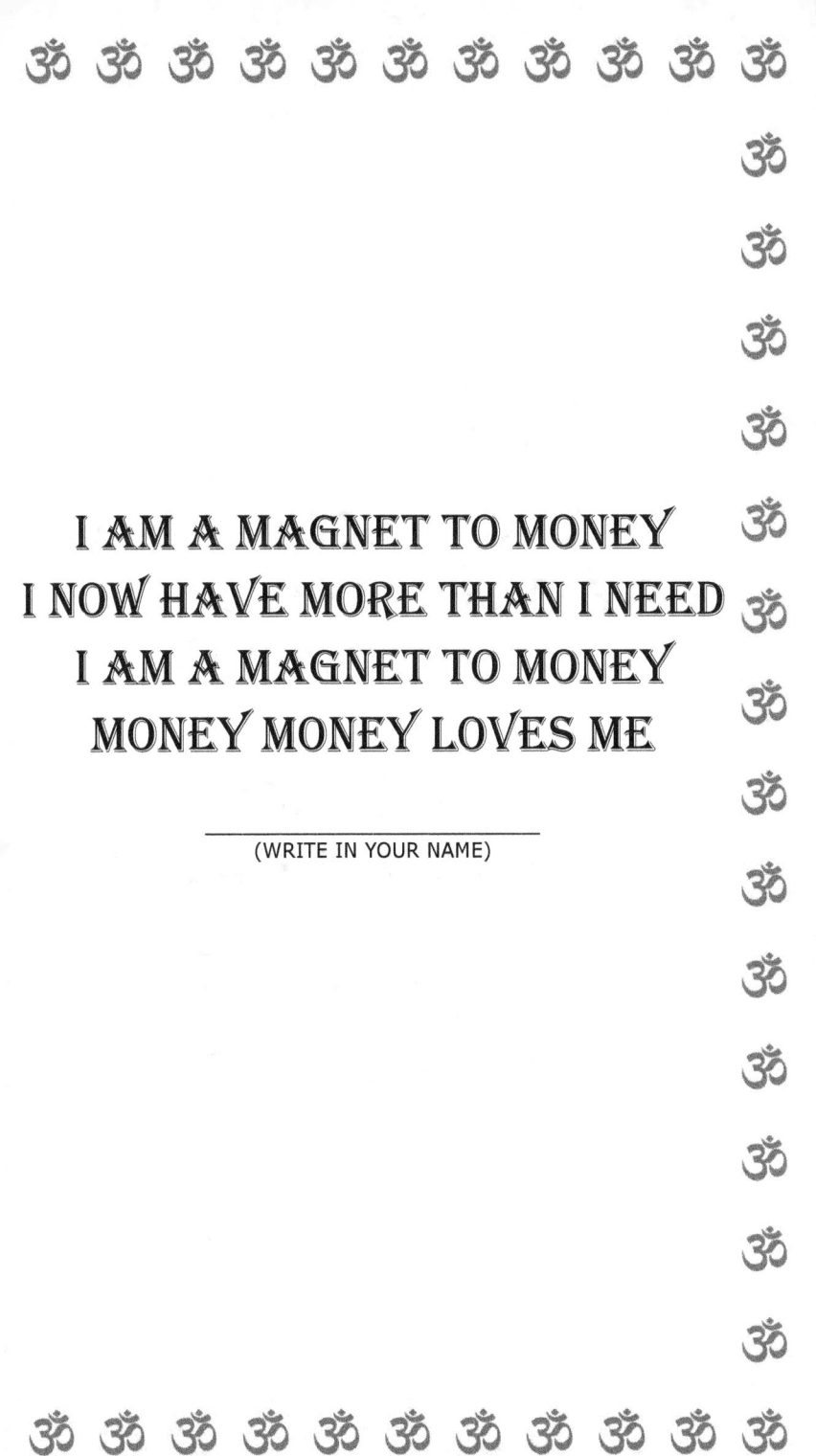

I LOVE AND ACCEPT MYSELF
AND EAT ONLY THE FOOD THAT
IS GOOD FOR ME

I AM ENERGY
I EXERCISE REGULARLY

MY BODY IS HEALTHY
I AM FULL OF LIFE,
I AM ENERGY

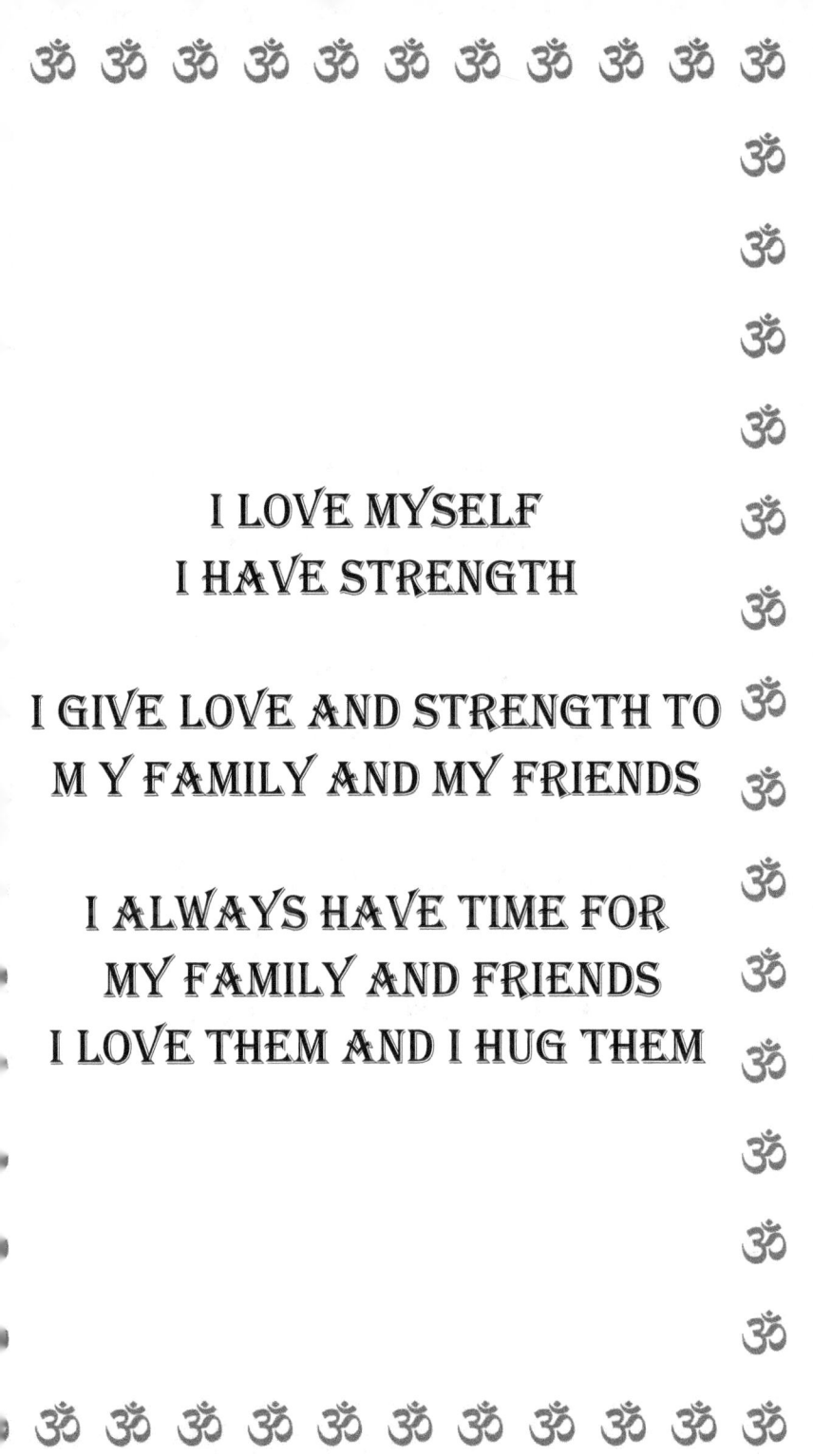

I LOVE MYSELF
I HAVE STRENGTH

I GIVE LOVE AND STRENGTH TO
MY FAMILY AND MY FRIENDS

I ALWAYS HAVE TIME FOR
MY FAMILY AND FRIENDS
I LOVE THEM AND I HUG THEM

I AM A MAGNET TO MONEY
IN ALL FORMS

MONEY IS MY
OBEDIENT SERVANT

I NOW ACHIEVE ALL OF MY
TRUE GOALS
AND I AM DEBT FREE

I NOW HAVE CLARITY CHOICE
AND TRUE MENTAL BALANCE

I AM NOW DEVELOPING MY
MIND WITH FURTHER
EDUCATION

I LOVE TO LOVE
AND I ALWAYS FORGIVE
I ONLY SPEAK THE TRUTH
THAT I LIVE

I AM LIVING MY LIFE
IN TRUE FREEDOM

I AM NOW ATTRACTING ALL
THE RIGHT PEOPLE INTO MY
LIFE WHO SUPPORT AND
STRENGTHEN MY SUCCESS
AS I ALSO LOVE
AND SUPPORT MY LOVED ONES

I AM A POWERFUL SPIRIT
LIVING IN A PHYSICAL BODY

MY SPIRIT IS ENDLESS DIVINE
ENERGY WITH AN ALL
CREATIVE MIND.

I NOW OPEN MYSELF TO THE
SPIRIT WITHIN KNOWING THAT
I AM BEING GUIDED TO
MY HIGHEST GOOD

TODAY I HAVE A BRAND NEW
GLOW FOR I AM ENERGY

I'M FULL OF LOVE
MY ACTIONS SHOW
THAT I AM ENERGY

I FEEL ALIVE, NOW I CAN SEE
A BRIGHTER FUTURE
IS HERE FOR ME
NOTHING CAN STOP ME NOW

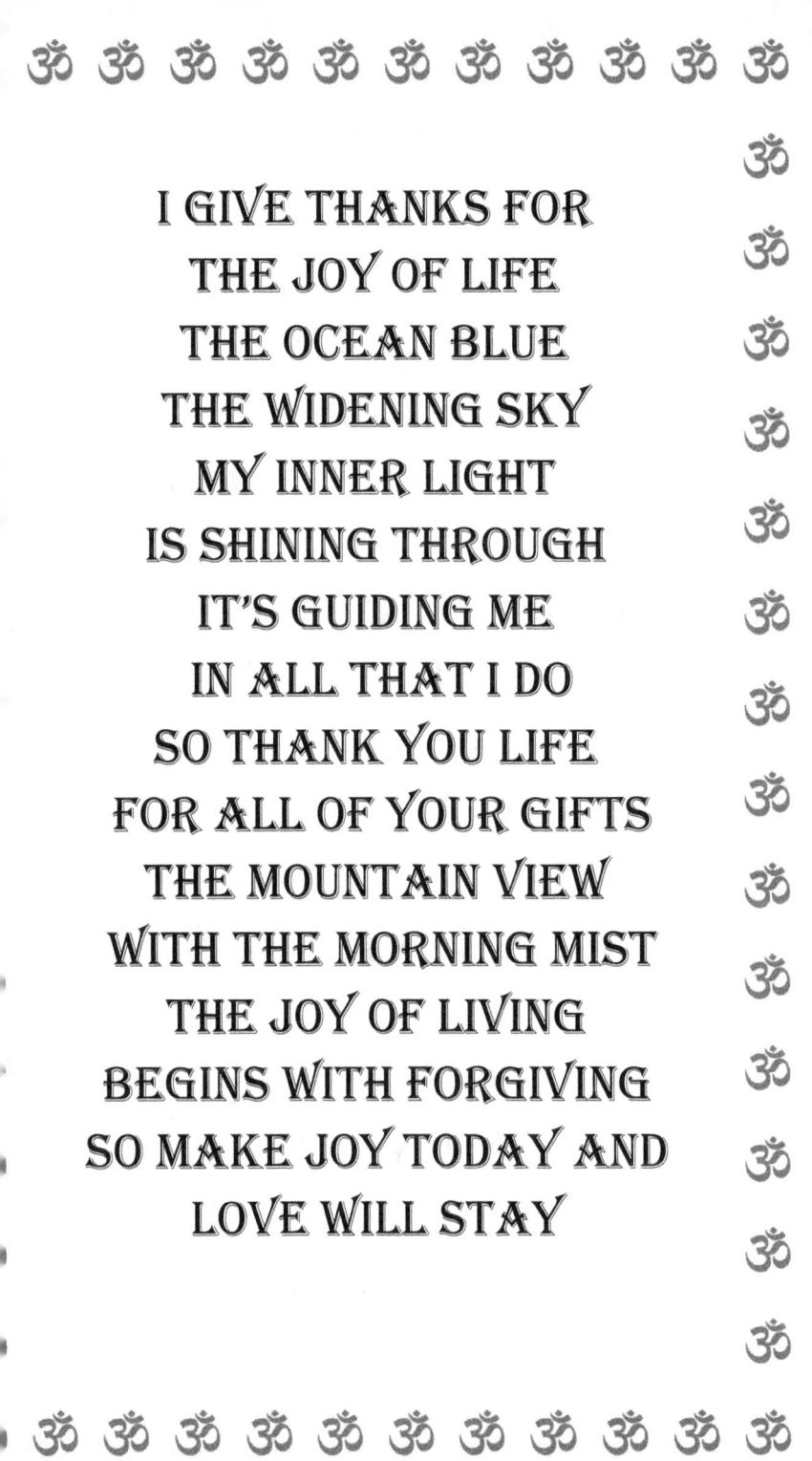

I GIVE THANKS FOR
THE JOY OF LIFE
THE OCEAN BLUE
THE WIDENING SKY
MY INNER LIGHT
IS SHINING THROUGH
IT'S GUIDING ME
IN ALL THAT I DO
SO THANK YOU LIFE
FOR ALL OF YOUR GIFTS
THE MOUNTAIN VIEW
WITH THE MORNING MIST
THE JOY OF LIVING
BEGINS WITH FORGIVING
SO MAKE JOY TODAY AND
LOVE WILL STAY

I LOVE MYSELF
TODAY RIGHT NOW
I FILL MY MIND AND FEELING
NATURE WITH LOVE
I GO FORWARD THIS DAY
WITH LOVE FOR ALL

I LOVE MY CUSTOMERS
I LOVE THEM ALL
I GIVE MY LOVE TO THEM
THEN I LOVE THEM SOME MORE

I REMEMBER ALL
THEIR NAMES
LOVE SHINES IN THEIR EYES
YES, I LOVE MY CUSTOMERS
FOR WE ARE ALL FROM
ONE MIND

I'M IN TOUCH WITH WHO I AM
I AM LOVE WOMAN & MAN
I'M IN TOUCH WITH WHO I AM
I AM LOVE

I'M IN TOUCH WITH WHO I AM
MOTHER NATURE IS MY LAND
I'M IN TOUCH WITH WHO I AM
I AM LOVE
I AM LOVE, I AM LOVE

I BELIEVE MY SOUL TO BE LIVING IN
GOD'S ENDLESS DREAM
I BELIEVE MY SOUL
BELIEVES IT IS LOVE

HEAL ME WITH YOUR GENTLE TOUCH
UNCONDITIONALLY
WITH YOUR TRUST
WARM AND TENDER
OH, I KNOW I AM LOVE

THIS IS NOW MY PERFECT DAY
PERFECT IN EVERY WAY
FILLED WITH RIGHT ACTION
FILLED WITH PERFECT TIMING

THIS IS NOW MY PERFECT DAY
PERFECT IN EVERY WAY
FILLED WITH RIGHT THINKING
FILLED WITH
PERFECT KNOWING
CRADLED IN THE ARMS OF
DIVINE INSPIRATION
I SEE THE DIVINE IN EVERYONE
I AM MEETING
THIS IS NOW MY PERFECT DAY

I AM NEVER LONELY
FOR THE SPIRIT LIVES IN ME

I AM NEVER LONELY
MY JOY HAS SET ME FREE

I AM NEVER LONELY
FOR I AM MY BEST FRIEND

I AM HEALED I KNOW I AM
I LOVE MYSELF I AM MY FRIEND
I TRUST MYSELF

I LOVE WHO I AM I AM HEALED
I KNOW I AM
I LOVE MYSELF
I AM MY FRIEND

AS THE HEALING LIGHT
OF THE UNIVERSE
SURROUNDS ME AND FLOWS
THROUGH ME
I KNOW THAT I AM HEALED

I AM NOT JUST MYSELF
I AM ONE WITH THE
WHOLE WORLD

DIVINE LOVE LIVES IN ME
SHINING RIGHT THROUGH
FOR ALL TO SEE

DIVINE LOVE GIVES TO ME
INNER PEACE AND HARMONY
YES, DIVINE LOVE LIVES IN ME

I AM PERFECT
I AM NOW PERFECT
WHO I AM IS DIVINE
THEREFORE I AM PERFECT

I AM NOW BEING WHO I AM
FOR I AM PERFECT
I AM PERFECT
I AM A CHILD OF GOD
MY DIVINE HERITAGE
IS PERFECTION

THERE ARE NO LIMITATIONS
JUST GIVE ME LIFE AND I WILL LIVE
JUST GIVE ME LOVE, I WILL FORGIVE
JUST GIVE ME AIR AND I WILL BREATHE
OH, I DO BELIEVE

DON'T GIVE ME LIMITATIONS
DON'T GIVE ME SAFETY NETS
DON'T GIVE ME PRISON WALLS
I WON'T SLEEP IN BURNING BEDS

JUST GIVE ME SUN AND I WILL SHINE
JUST GIVE ME BREAD
GRAPES FROM THE VINE
GIVE ME FAITH AND I'LL RECEIVE
O I DO BELIEVE

WON'T LISTEN TO WHAT THEY SAY
WON'T BE JUST LIKE THE REST
WON'T BE A PART OF THEIR PLAY
JUST WANT TO BE MY BEST
I AM UNLIMITED
THERE ARE NO LIMITATIONS IN MY LIFE

I AM STRONG
I AM BEAUTIFUL

I ONLY ATTRACT
GOOD IN MY LIFE

ALL OF MY RELATIONSHIPS
ARE PERFECT
FOR TRUST BEGINS WITH ME
ALL OF MY RELATIONSHIPS
ARE PERFECT
FOR LOVE IS ALWAYS FREE

I TRUST MYSELF
I LOVE WHO I AM
MY RELATIONSHIPS WITH
MYSELF IS PERFECT
FOR I AM ONE WITH
THE ETERNAL DIVINE

WHEN LIFE CLOSES A DOOR
A WINDOW ALWAYS OPEN
WHEN LIFE PUTS YOU TO THE TEST
IT'S A CHANGE TO BE YOUR BEST
THE LESSONS YOU MUST LEARN
WILL NEVER BURN
JUST LEARN TO LOVE
AND YOU'LL HAVE YOUR TURN

I KNOW THAT WE WERE BORN
TO SCARE THE LONELINESS AWAY
SO IF YOU WANT TO REACH ME
THEN YOU'VE GOT TO TEACH ME
IF YOU WANT TO REACH ME
TEACH ME ABOUT LOVE

NEVER TOO YOUNG TO SHOW YOU CARE
NEVER TOO OLD
YOU'VE JUST GOT TO BE AWARE
IN QUIET MOMENTS, LOOK TO YOUR SOUL
AND THEN TOGETHER
WE'LL KEEP OUT THE COLD
I AM NOW REACHING MY FULL POTENTIAL
AS I LEARN TO LOVE

I LIVE TO LOVE
AND ALWAYS FORGIVE
I ALWAYS FORGIVE
I ONLY SPEAK THE TRUTH
THAT I LIVE
THE TRUTH THAT I LIVE

I FORGIVE EVERYONE
AND EVERYTHING
KNOWING THAT WE ARE ALL
DOING THE BEST WE CAN
WITH WHAT WE KNOW
RIGHT NOW
I FORGIVE MYSELF
THEREFORE I AM FORGIVEN

THE SPIRITUAL BEING
THAT I AM
IS ALREADY AWAKENED

I AM PURE
DIVINE CONSCIOUSNESS
AND I AM ALREADY
ETERNALLY FREE

I AM AN INFINITE
BEING OF LIGHT

I AM ONE WITH THE GREATEST
SOURCE OF DIVINE LOVE
AND LOVE IS THE
ONLY TRUE POWER

THE ETERNAL HOLY LIGHT IS GENEROUS, GIVING & LOVING

MY HIGHER SELF IS
PURE INTUITION
THEREFORE I ALWAYS KNOW
WHAT TO DO AND WHAT TO SAY
IN EVERY MOMENT
AND IN EVERY SITUATION

MY HIGHER SELF IS GOOD LOVING
GENTLE AND PURE

I LOVE THE ETERNAL IN EVERYBODY UNCONDITIONALLY

MY SPIRIT UPLIFTS
AND INSPIRES OTHERS

I AM NOW SO VERY HEALTHY
AS MY SPIRIT HAS INSPIRED ME
TO WORK OUT

I FEEL BETTER AND BETTER AND
HEALTHIER AND HEALTHIER EVERY
SINGLE DAY

I ALWAYS TAKE
RIGHT DIVINE ACTION

ALL IN MY LIFE
IS IN RIGHT DIVINE ORDER

I LOVE MY LIFE

I LOVE THE DIVINE MORE AND MORE IN
EVERY MOMENT

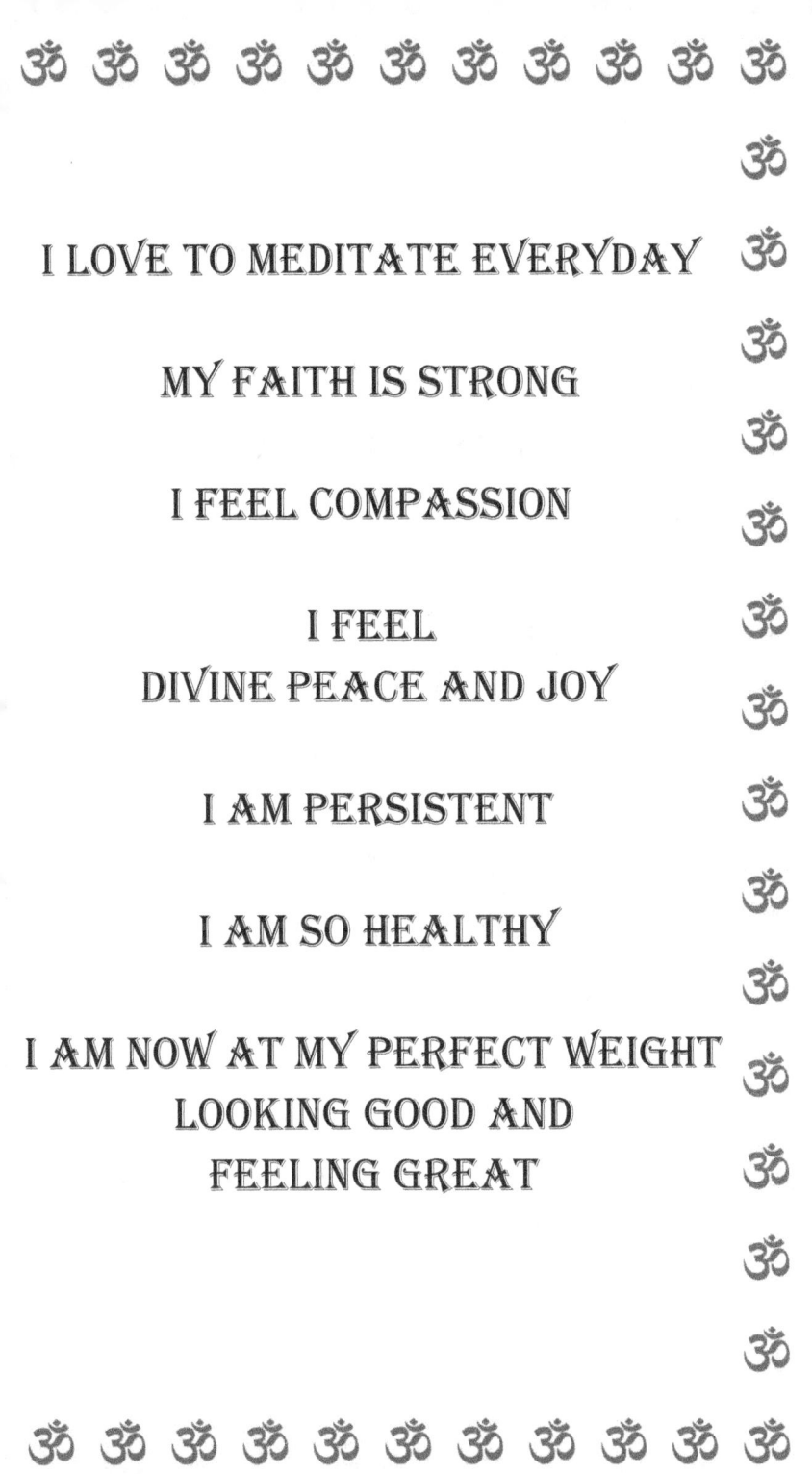

I AM THE FITTEST AND
HEALTHIEST OF MY LIFE

EVERY DAY IN EVERY
DIVINE RIGHT WAY
I AM HEALTHIER AND HEALTHIER

EVERY DAY IN EVERY
DIVINE RIGHT WAY
I AM BETTER AND BETTER

EVERY DAY IN EVERY
DIVINE RIGHT WAY
I AM HAPPIER AND HAPPIER

EVERY DAY IN EVERY
DIVINE RIGHT WAY
I AM FITTER AND FITTER

EVERY DAY IN EVERY
DIVINE RIGHT WAY
I AM RICHER AND RICHER...

RICHER IN MONEY
RICHER IN HEALTH
RICHER IN FAITH
RICHER IN LOVE
RICHER IN MEDITATION
RICHER IN PEACE
AND RICHER IN
DIVINE FRIENDSHIP

I ALWAYS TAKE RIGHT DIVINE
ACTION THAT ASSISTS
MY MEDITATION PRACTICE

MY MEDITATION PRACTICE IS
BECOMING DEEPER
AND DEEPER

MY FAMILY IS UPLIFTED
MY HEALTH IS GLOWING

I AM CALM AND FILLED WITH
OVERFLOWING PEACE

I LOVE YOU, GOD,
I KNOW ALL THINGS
ARE POSSIBLE WITH YOU

I AM SUBMERGED
IN ETERNAL HOLY LIGHT

I LOVE TO MEDITATE EVERY DAY

MAY THERE ALWAYS BE MORE OF
GOD IN ME THAN ME

HOLY LIGHT PERMEATES EVERY
PARTICLE OF MY BEING

I AM LIVING IN THAT LIGHT
I AM THE HOLY LIGHT

DIVINE SPIRIT FILLS ME WITHIN
AND WITHOUT

I AM 100% GOD GOVERNED

I AM ENLIGHTENMENT

ENLIGHTENMENT
IS OMNIPRESENT

OM MANI PADME HUM

THANK YOU DIVINE FOR THIS
BEAUTIFUL HAPPY HEALTHY
PROSPEROUS FULFILLING LIFE

THE MYSTICAL EXPERIENCE™
www.TheMysticalExperience.com

Vibrate at a higher frequency.
Ignite Your True Unlimited Potential and
Experience Success in Life Through
Transformation of Consciousness
with this life changing platform.
Since 2005 transforming
thousands of lives.

How can we transform our lives?

Through transforming our consciousness. Can we do this alone? Yes, however it is a very difficult path to do alone. Here at the Mystical Experience you are prayed for every single day and sent transmissions of Light Energy (Shakti).

Here in the Mystical Experience it is our goal and positive intention to strip away old paradigms of false beliefs and become one with our true Higher Self. And hence our Divine Destiny is at last revealed in all its glory! There is much given through this membership in Divine vibrational energy transmissions, exercises, live stream events and more.

Do you wish to have harmony, happiness and fulfilling success? You can wake up to who you truly are. ALL things are possible. The natural evolution for all sentient beings and that means YOU, is ENLIGHTENMENT! If you feel you want evolution in all areas of you life then watch our FREE videos at...

www.TheMysticalExperience.com

HERE IS YOUR OPPORTUNITY TO WRITE DOWN YOUR OWN AFFIRMATIONS AND RECORD THEM WITH YOUR OWN VOICE

REMEMBER TO PERSONALIZE THEM
AND WRITE THEM IN THE NOW
SPEAK AND SING YOUR AFFIRMATIONS
WITH EMOTION AND LOVE. AND ABOVE ALL HAVE FUN

WRITE AND SPEAK YOUR AFFIRMATIONS A MINIMUM OF TEN TIMES AS THEN THE SUBCONSCIOUS BEGINS TO BELIEVE
IT IS THE TRUTH FOR YOU RIGHT NOW
YOU WILL BE FILLED WITH MAGNETIC POWER

SAY RIGHT NOW

I AM FILLED WITH MAGNETIC POWER.
I ONLY ATTRACT GOOD IN MY LIFE

MY PHYSICAL AFFIRMATIONS

MY MIND AFFIRMATIONS

MY FINANCIAL AFFIRMATIONS

MY SOCIAL AFFIRMATIONS

MY FAMILY AFFIRMATIONS

MY TRAVEL AFFIRMATIONS

MY SPIRITUAL AFFIRMATIONS

MY CAREER AFFIRMATIONS

MY GLOBAL AFFIRMATIONS

MY MATERIAL AFFIRMATIONS

MY PHYSICAL GOALS

FULL Audio version of this Powerful book spoken by the authors with added extras is available at
www.MusiVation.com

www.EMusiVation.com

**Or from Amazon.com, Barnes & Noble, Borders and all good bookstores worldwide!
For wholesale orders of this book email us at:**
Team@TheMysticalExperience.com

Our Main Websites

www.TheMagicOfAffirmationPower.com

www.TheMysticalExperience.com

For our entire success catalog go to:
www.MusiVation.com

For positive and motivational ringtones go to:
www.RingtonesForSuccess.com

What others are saying about
www.TheMysticalExperience.com **and Michele Blood...**

"Michele Blood is truly a special person. For over three decades, I have made a serious study of the mind and how to live a full and balanced life. I have taught tens of thousands of people around the world how to properly utilize their God-given potential, and then along came Michele Blood. She had a very positive impact on my life, for which I am truly grateful! She made me aware of unique methods for realizing more power by effectively combining affirmations and music. Invest in her entire library and let this petite powerhouse show you a fast and effective way to enjoy more of life's rich rewards. I enthusiastically introduce Michele Blood and her wonderful work to every audience. Order her material today! Share Michele and her MusiVation™ discovery with your world; they will thank you with sincere gratitude."
- Bob Proctor, Author of the Best-Selling Book "You Were Born Rich"

"Michele has combined the essence of two great ideas; music and autosuggestion. Autosuggestion has long been recognized as a powerful motivational tool and music has inspired every generation for centuries. In her singing affirmations Michele combines the two and shares the power that has propelled her to great success, power that can help you motivate yourself to the highest levels of achievement. Michele belongs to every achiever's tape library."
- Samuel A. Cypert, Author of "Achieve & Believe"

Dearest Michele, I want to say Thank You So Much for all that you're doing for the Mystical Experience people. You've made my life alive again. Thank you, Thank you...
- Patti C.

Being introduced to Michele's Mystical Experience has changed my life for the best. I can get the most powerful, up-lifting and energizing emotions when I participate in any of Michele's in-person or live stream teachings. My life has been so hectic over the past few months, but I make it my priority to spend time listening and learning from Michele, because she brings my life back into absolute consciousness. I appreciate and treasure the time Michele dedicates to helping those who are searching for their higher self. I absolutely feel I achieve a higher consciousness with each and every one of Michele's sessions. Thank you, thank you, thank you.... I am gaining momentum to my higher self, to reaching my unlimited consciousness. God Bless You Michele.
- Don Runowski

When Michele first prayed for me and gave me specific instructions to feel the stillness within I was in over $500,000 credit card debt in just 4 months I was out of debt through a totally unexpected gift. I feel free and happy and am now also in a new Beautiful relationship with someone who really gets me.
- J'En El, Author/speaker

I am blown away with Michele's enthusiasm and genuine energy she is able to project. I have followed her work and Bob Proctors for years. In the past year I received and email about a seminar she was holding and I attended and was blown away. It seemed to fit into everything I had always known the theory of what my own mystical projects were about. Now I'm a member of her Mystical Success Club with ongoing Light Transmissions, monthly DVD's and weekly webinars. I find this a rare way to evolve and to stay current. This club is helping me stay true to purpose, direction; I am growing in knowledge and light experience with someone who has years of success as an author, mentor, musician, career coach, and mystic etc. and I LOVE IT!

Thank you Michele!
- Kim Ripley Hartt, Author of Mysticism

Michele's insights, music and exploration into the mystical success we can tap into through her Mystical Experience website and many other products and books takes all that she has to offer to help with the richness of her transformational teachings. I loved the club and the monthly DVD's are pouring with energy transmission. I highly recommend it as a priceless sacred space for you to grow in consciousness and to bring harmony to all of your family members
- Bernadette Dimitrov Author for Children's books

Dear Michele, It is with a heart full of gratitude that I am writing this email tonight. I've just finished watching the meditation DVD, and for that I am grateful. Your face shines because of the Love and Gratitude that you have for the Divine/God. And your Prayer recording also made a major shift in my heart. The words cannot describe how grateful I am to have found you when I did. My prayers to God were to end my life if I had to continue living the same way. For without God in my life, I am nothing. And I forgot to listen to my heart and more importantly I forgot the main ingredient: GRATITUDE. You have opened my eyes as to why I lost my Faith. And dear Michele I have to thank you for having restored my Faith in the Divine/God. I have re-gained something priceless: my Faith. It is so true that in every minute of our lives, we have to choose thoughts that will determine our future.
- J. Marie

A quick note Michele to let you know that I had one of the best weeks in a long time. I am on a very large global computer system project that has a lot of negative energy associated with it because of the perceived time constraints with the amount of work to do. Many of the people on this project are frustrated

which I was one of them until this past week. I believe it was the prayer you did for me last Saturday that changed my energy levels and something else in me. I am at peace, energized and very positive knowing things will work out. A big change from where I used to operate because I worried, stressed on time deadlines for many years. It lets me think more clearly now, probably more creative but it has only been a week. I feel transformed.
- **Gary B.**

Thank you so much Michelle. You did prayers for me last Christmas and almost everything came true!! It has been a blessed year.
- **L. Cash**

Michele, The Mystical Experience and your prayers have done SO MUCH for my life! There has been so much I appreciate of all of your work and love. Being part of this club had healed so many wounds that my past had left me with, and it has allowed me to move forward so much in bravery and perseverance. As a member, I feel so honored to be part of such beautiful love. Never in my life have I felt so close to a circle of such open and loving people. Being part of the mystical path had broken so many of the restricting chains of resistance I had. I was caught up in a mess of a depression so painful I had lost almost all sanity, yet something just kept telling me "Keep strong and keep believing, what you're looking for is just around the corner". I knew this was where true light was and what it really meant to feel freedom. Or rather FREED- OMMMMMMM! I can't seem to find any words to describe this feeling. Thank you Michele for every single thing you've given me. Thank you, thank you, thank you, and may you be blessed with all of my love. Thank you. I LOVE YOU!
- **Elida, NY**

Michele, I wanted to thank you again for who you are and what you do. God has given to the world a special gift with you. He is truly working through you. It's been about two weeks now since I was on the special prayer call that you opened up to many people. Thank you for doing that! Since then I have joined the Mystical Experience, I continue to live each day with much more joy and happiness and I know I am just beginning my way to being one with the universe in consciousness, one with everyone and everything. I feel like I am being reborn and my consciousness is awakening. I have been living unconsciously almost my whole life, although I knew there was something waiting to bust out but didn't know how to do it. I know God wants to use me and I yearn for that. He has brought me to you to make this happen. Lots of Energy and Love.
- **George B.**

Dear Michele, Your prayers helped me to find a job working with developmentally disabled Souls. So many Miracles! Bless you so much! With Love and Light.
- **Caroline**

Thank you, Michele, since I joined www.TheMysticalExperience.com I've been feeling my heart open more and more, thank you for that! I want to share something with you, it's an experience that filled my being with joy. Today, I was walking down the street, thinking about something you said on one of the weekly webinars - you said that there is logic language, and then there is love language. And there and then, I realized — love language is wordless! It's everything, and everywhere, it's all around me! It's the trees standing by the roadside, it's the air around us, its people, unconnected, all over the world, just doing anything — walking, sleeping, eating, breathing... I am love language, I am love language speaking itself through me. Even logic language is love, it is not apart from it, it couldn't exist if not for love! All of this, all of us, we are the language of love.

And it is being spoken, all the time, everyday…. I couldn't not speak it. I couldn't not hear it. Thank you for giving me this experience, it is this that I have been yearning for so long. I knew I knew this someplace, somewhere, I had just forgotten for a little while.
- **Yen L.**

I just wanted to tell you that I have received what I asked for in the prayer request I sent you and to tell you what happened, it is very interesting! I had sent in a request prayer for my sister Diane to find a job and a place to live (they were staying with me since they moved to CA) Well Michele, today they picked up the keys to their apartment and will be moving within this week! My prayer was answered!
- **Vicky W.**

My dear Michele, Thank you very much for your priceless energy transformation. Since Sunday my husband has been transforming in a good way. After a really long time he is interested in me again and hugs me kisses me and I can see the love in his eyes. This is like miracle and how much I appreciate your help!!! Thank you very much again for all your help. God bless you.
- **Yonca**

Dearest Angel Michele. Very fast miracle after your Light Transmission. The transfer I wanted to Kochin City came in 20 hours later. It's incredibly beautiful. It has to be felt to be believed. I am grateful for your kind blessed light. Improved my health also. Thanking your beautiful soul. Tour energy par compare.
- **Sreekanth, India**

www.ingramcontent.com/pod-product-compliance
Lightning Source LLC
Chambersburg PA
CBHW070951080526
44587CB00015B/2253